# Unleash Your Investments

## 9 Simple Truths to Transform your Legacy

Published by Outspoken Fiduciary Publishing, LLC

Printed in the United States of America.

ISBN-13: 978-1537358246

ISBN-10: 1537358243

Additional copies are available at special quantity discounts for bulk purchases for sales promotions, premiums, fundraising, and educational use.

For more information, please contact:

Outspoken Fiduciary Publishing, **480-782-1034**

Contact the author directly at info@keystonewealthpartners.com

*This book is dedicated to*
*My bride, Brittany.*

*From the moment we met,*
*you challenged me*
*to dream bigger dreams,*
*and pursue more in life*
*than I thought was possible.*
*Thank you for your loyalty,*
*trust, and encouragement.*

# Contents

# Acknowledgements and Credits

Looking at my professional journey thus far, there have been several influential people whose footprints I followed.

Without my father-in-law, Larry Warren, I would have never been exposed to the financial industry and would probably still be flying commercial airliners. He not only gave me a vision for what it meant to guide people with their investment planning, but also voiced an unwavering confidence in my ability to build a business from scratch in Arizona, as a new adviser in my 20's. Early in my career, his encouraging words spurred me to continue my pursuit to help people plan for a comfortable retirement even when it seemed to me like I was swimming upstream.

My father, Tom Hagensen, has had a huge impact on me in a multitude of ways. It was he who taught me about business ethics. He encouraged me to pursue my dreams of being an entrepreneur and impressed the importance of consistency, follow-through, hard work, and integrity.

Paul Bennett, a Managing Director at United Capital in Great Falls, Virginia was willing to mentor me when I had little to offer the industry, and certainly nothing to offer an experienced, successful adviser like him in return for his guidance. Regardless, he was always willing to answer the phone when I called, and for that I will forever be grateful. He modeled for me the importance of being a constant learner and how vital it is for my clients that I remain at the top of my game and an expert in my field.

Furthermore, Paul's entrepreneurial courage led him to operate as a fee-only fiduciary, long before it was popular and expected. His disciplined, cerebral approach to financial planning, as well as emphasis on investor behavior, helped shape many of the ways we help clients today.

Lastly, I want to acknowledge Ric Edelman. I have admired him from afar. He is one of the true pioneers for what it means to be an independent financial adviser. Through the years I have read many of his books and listened to thousands of hours of his podcast and radio show. Ric exemplifies what it means to educate investors so that they can make prudent decisions with what they have worked so hard for.

Although I would love to claim that the themes of this book encompass ideas that no one has ever considered, spoken, or written about before, the reality is that these influencers above, in addition to countless others not listed, have formed me as an adviser and in turn, have inspired the words in this book. Without so many people who have selflessly poured their knowledge and experience into me, I would not be where I am today, and this book would not exist. I hope my life, business, and to a lesser degree, this book, represents all those mentors well.

# Introduction

**By John Hagensen**

Over the past nine decades, the stock market has provided Americans with a rollercoaster ride that would rival anything Magic Mountain has to offer. During the year-to-year yo-yos we've experienced, spikes, flash-crashes, and market corrections. We have endured Jimmy Carter's presidency as well as near 0% fed funds rates. There have been recessions, depressions, national tragedies, World Wars, times of great celebration, prolonged "bear markets", and plenty of sustained "bull markets." Because we are human beings, we are influenced by all of these cycles, and have an uncanny propensity for acting upon our short-term emotions. Unfortunately, research tells us that the majority of us make poor investment decisions that carry long-term consequences during times of heightened emotions.

There are two goals I have for you as you read this book. My first is that you feel validated by what I teach you. Through empirical evidence and data, I will outline several facts about money and investing, and I am hopeful that much of it will be an affirmation of what you have always known to be true. However, be warned, this book is not all rainbows and unicorns. My second goal is equally as important: that you will begin to question what you have mistakenly believed as truth for many years. It is through this maturation that you may be empowered and equipped to create the lasting legacy you have always dreamed of.

Someone I respect once told me what *I believe to be true* is irrelevant. Instead, he told me that what really matters is *what, in fact, is true*. Right now, I want to pass this same credo on to you.

I wrote this book to change your legacy, not to make you feel comfortable with the status quo. Some of what you read might test your ego and shatter your "old way of doing things". Don't worry, you'll be okay. Recognize that growth only occurs through trial, perseverance, and progression. The financial community has perpetuated many ideas over the years (absent from facts or data) yet we have been conditioned to blindly believe them as truth. Throughout the pages of this book I will carefully dissect the ideas often responsible for destroying Main Street Investors' financial freedom and nuke those myths into outer space.

There is always talk about the world's anomalous people who strike lightning in a bottle. You can't walk through a Barnes and Noble without seeing the faces of these so-called "gurus" gracing magazine covers. Still, the fact remains that there is no "magic algorithm" or "proprietary strategy" certain to bring instant riches upon you. Instead, I will share with you an efficient methodology for growing wealth that is academically, historically, and statistically validated – and no, it doesn't involve taking out a second mortgage to buy Bitcoin!

Imagine: What if the success of your financial dreams didn't hinge on forecasting, stock picking, or track-record investing? What if your success didn't require the educated guess of a commission-driven broker, or hundreds of hours of personal investment research?

**What if, instead, you had a defined and stated investment philosophy to guide all of your financial decisions?**

I have made it my professional mission to teach investors the truth of proper investing. For whatever reason, we have been blessed as Americans with more riches than any society in the world's history.

In light of that fact, I stand convinced that it is my moral obligation to provide you an awareness of how to prudently manage that wealth to which you have been entrusted. This is a task that I take on with great pride and responsibility.

I wrote this book to serve as a catalyst as you begin your journey toward finding clarity and contentment with your money. I hope that it provides you with perspective and renews your optimism for realizing your financial goals. If you're willing and able, join me on a journey through these 9 simple truths that will transform your legacy.

*"Without counsel plans fail, but with many advisers they succeed." Proverbs 15:22*

# Chapter One:
# Simple Rules Are Hard to Follow

Have you ever noticed in life that often times some of the simplest concepts to understand are the most difficult to follow? Investing isn't a whole lot different and it perfectly reflects that life truth. While the rules for investing aren't all that complicated, following them can be very, very difficult - even over short periods of time. What's exponentially more difficult, is following these rules consistently over a lifetime.

There are many examples of this concept in day-to-day life. One of the simplest to grasp is losing weight and maintaining a physically fit body. Most anyone will agree the rules of losing weight are simple to understand: eat less, move more. These are two simple, very basic rules. We ALL know the challenge of losing weight has very little to do with knowing or understanding the rules for living a fit life. Everyone has the desire to have six-pack abs.

*We all want it. We all know HOW to be fit. So why isn't everyone in tip-top shape?*

The difference between knowing all of the rules and following them is HUGE.

Consistently following what we know to be true—over long periods of time—is not easy at all. In fact, it is VERY, VERY difficult. Hence, this is the reason why everyone isn't an underwear model.

Investing is a whole lot of the same idea. Like the rules for being fit, the rules of investing are simple to understand, but are equally as difficult to follow. In this chapter, I will teach you the simple rules of investing. However, don't forget the "Eat Less, Move More" rule. Learning the rules and following them are two entirely separate skills. In fact, if you know the rules of investing, you are unfortunately no more prone to being a successful investor. Instead, it's only when you FOLLOW the rules that success will be yours. That conviction and discipline will also reap true confidence and peace of mind surrounding your money.

We have been misled to believe that clearing our proverbial "investment hurdles" depends primarily on knowing how to invest. Stockbrokers and traditional financial advisers have taught us that the only path to complete understanding is through a submission to them and their firms. They have focused their sales process on their extensive knowledge of these rules, while failing to help you actually understand them for yourself, or more importantly, help you follow them.

We've all been told the same myth. Now, get ready for the truth. The biggest value of a true financial adviser is to be your accountability partner and guide. An adviser's primary role is to help you follow those rules over long periods of time. As your "Sherpa," a good financial coach is tasked with continually providing you tools to remain on course.

Remember the fitness comparison? What if Celebrity Trainer Jillian Michaels picked you up every single day at 5 a.m. and presented a workout routine just for you.

She would take you each day to the gym, providing oversight for everything you ate and for every workout activity. In three years you would look at yourself in the mirror and say, "Wow, I am looking pretty darn good!" You would think to yourself, "I FEEL GREAT!"

Did your transformation occur because Jillian Michaels explained the benefits of exercise and healthy eating to you? No. You already knew the basic rules of a healthy lifestyle. The difference in this scenario is that Jillian Michaels walked you through, hand-in-hand, picking you up every morning while holding you accountable. It is not enough simply to KNOW the rules, living them is the only thing that achieves desired results. Investing and financial planning works in the very same way.

**Here are the three basic rules to a sound investment strategy:**

1. **Own equities.**
2. **Diversify.**
3. **Rebalance.**

To become and remain a successful investor, you need only to follow these three rules and repeat them throughout the rest of your life. Simple right?

To help you understand, let's unpack each rule.

**Rule number one:** Own equities.

In simple terms, there is significant risk in buying individual stocks because each individual company bears its own risk. Similarly, active mutual funds have their own series of problems.

I'll cover stock picking and mutual funds a little later in the book, however I want to be clear that I do not advocate owning equities in either of those two ways. Instead, I recommend investing in passively managed, low cost, highly diversified, mutual funds and exchange-traded funds (ETFs). Experience and data tells us that this strategy may be the most efficient way to own equities.

The first reason is that passive funds have lower than average internal expenses and possess more holdings - meaning they are cheaper and more diversified. Another reason to utilize them is that they are typically lower in turnover ratios - meaning when they appear in taxable accounts they're much more tax efficient. Last but not least, they outperform active, antiquated retail mutual funds the vast majority of the time. Ultimately the stock market has earned over 10% per year since 1926, and owning equities is a critical foundation to almost all financial plans.

**Rule number two:** Diversify.

Diversification is a buzzword heard far too often within investment circles. It is almost obnoxious how frequently this word is slung around. What does it even mean? Let me first explain what it *doesn't* mean.

It does not mean, "own a bunch of stuff." Too many people believe if they simply own several different investments within their accounts, then they are diversified. This is not even remotely true.

Diversification is a scientific process. In 1990, Dr. Harry Markowitz was awarded the Nobel Prize for his work on Modern Portfolio Theory – which is the foundational basis for diversification.

You see, diversification is actually an academic exercise that correlates one asset class to another with the result being a collection of assets that move differently in relation to the others. Building a portfolio that falls on a Markowitz Efficient Frontier curve is a wise process - I'll get into that a little later on in this book as well.

Practically speaking, diversification means owning investments that rarely move the same as other investments you own. This dissimilar movement is what creates safety and volatility-dampening.

In review, follow rule number one by owning equities, and follow rule number two by making sure you diversify correctly. When nearing retirement, part of the diversification process may mean an investment in fewer equities because of their short-term unpredictability and volatility. As you grow closer to requiring use of your money, say within 10-years, it is vital to allocate money to vehicles that are safer and will help tamp down the volatility of your equities.

**Rule number three:** Rebalance.

This is the key. Rule three is the glue that keeps a plan anchored over long periods of time. As investors, our goal is always to buy low and sell high. Everyone knows that, but knowing and doing are two very different things – as mentioned earlier this chapter. Everyone wants to find the right stocks or choose the optimum time to jump in or out of the market. However, these attempts to buy low and sell high leave us with nothing more than anxiety and diminished investment returns over our lifetimes.

This is where rebalancing changes everything. When you rebalance a portfolio that has been well diversified, not only do you take advantage of the dissimilar price movement, but you are also are able to sell asset classes that have performed better – at a premium – and use those "strong dollars" to purchase asset classes that have performed worse – at a discount. The investments are still well diversified and there is no guessing whether to be in or out, or to weigh which asset classes to buy.

Rebalancing means never having to forecast which investments will perform better. Instead, a properly diversified and rebalanced portfolio takes advantage of the price chasm. There is tremendous confidence found when you know that you are ALWAYS selling high and ALWAYS buying low, without ever needing to *guess correctly ahead of time.*

This all sounds perfect, so what's the challenge? Here it is. As investors, we tend to desire the exact opposite. The last thing that we inherently want to do is purchase more of what is doing the poorest in our portfolio. Similarly, none of us naturally want to sell the asset that is up in value and performing best in our portfolio – especially to use the proceeds to buy our worst investment categories over the recent past. Our emotions play tricks on us.

# Emotions are our greatest flaw.

Studies reveal that a basic stock portfolio comprising of the 500 largest U.S. stocks has earned over 10% per year for the past 30 years. Conversely, the average stock mutual fund investor in the United States has earned just north of 3 percent during that same time frame. This sad reality demonstrates how difficult it is to follow these three basic rules.

Rebalancing is a difficult thing to live by - not because it isn't logical or our minds can't comprehend it – but because our emotions simply challenge us at every turn.

The apostle Paul says in Romans: "I do what I do not want to do, and I do not do want I want to do." It's good to know this confounding problem has been around at least a couple thousand years. It's perplexing. Everyone knows the rules –intellectually- of losing weight and becoming physically fit. It's simple, right? Eat less, move more. It is easy to follow rules for a day or so, but over a longer period of time, our level of discipline falls and we weaken. Investing is no different. It requires unwavering discipline.

Know these three rules. Follow them. Fight the urge to stray from them. Remain steadfast and the investment returns are phenomenal. Had you followed these rules the past 40 years, an initial investment of $100,000 would have grown to just under $5,000,000. There is no need to pick the right stocks or guess when to be in and when to be out of the market. Simply build a properly diversified portfolio and rebalance it regularly. That's it. It's that simple.

*Inspiration from the writings of Ric Edelman.*

## Chapter #1 – End of Chapter Questions

Have you found these rules difficult to follow over the years? If so, why?

_____

_____

_____

_____

_____

_____

Have you felt like your emotions have made it difficult for you to stay disciplined to a long-term strategy? If so, why and how?

_____

_____

_____

_____

_____

_____

_____

_____

_____

_____

# Chapter Two:
# The Four Landmines

In this chapter, I am addressing the four biggest landmines that challenge our investment goals. These landmines represent the four obstacles that most often impede progress.

Have you already figured out these four landmines? Typical guesses are Wall Street, the economy, natural disasters, taxes, the political climate, fees, commissions, and bad brokers.

**Nope, not even close. Not one.**

In fact, my experience as a financial planner having worked with countless investors tells me that in reality, the biggest threat to your own success is, well, it's YOU.

Ric Edelman, a financial adviser I greatly respect, has written and spoke about these four obstacles for decades as well. Here they are:

**Landmine Number One:** Procrastination

Raise your hand if you are a human being. For those reading that are in fact human, emotions are what set us apart from the animal kingdom. As human beings, our actions and behaviors are almost always influenced by our emotions. One of the biggest challenges we have in controlling our behavior is our inability to take action. We are all procrastinators.

The first landmine in our path is procrastination - an important obstacle that stands in our way.

To really understand the impact of procrastination, let's reflect on the story of a typical brother and sister.

Their names are Cruz and Zaya. Now Cruz was always a little bit unpredictable, while Zaya was a model of consistency and stability.

When Cruz started working at age 18, he decided to start saving $5,000 a year in an IRA. After about eight years, being the free-sprit personality he was, he stopped on a whim so that he could rekindle his love for collecting rare baseball cards. Now, you can see that Cruz was very ambitious, at first. During that time, Cruz squirreled away $40,000 total in savings.

After this, Cruz never saved again for the rest of his life. On the other hand, Cruz's sister, Zaya, was as disciplined as the very word itself. Zaya was on her path to becoming an attorney, and when she finished law school and passed the bar exam, she started saving at the age 26. Just as her brother had, she saved $5,000 per year. And she did it again, the next year, and the next year, until she had saved for 40 consecutive years. Zaya saved from age 26, every year, until age 65. Her total investment was $200,000.

**Who had more money-Cruz or Zaya--by age 65? Let's assume that they earned the same rates of return.**

Logically, if both earned a 10% rate of return, which is the approximate value that large U.S. stocks have made, according to Ibbotson and Associates, since 1927, do you think the answer would be "Zaya" since she saved $200,000 in comparison to Cruz's paltry $40,000?

**If you guessed Zaya you'd be wrong. Really? Yes.**

Zaya's investments totaled $2,212,963. Cruz's totaled $2,587,899. Their investment earnings reflect a $374,936 difference in Cruz's favor. How can that be?

This example is a demonstration of how impactful the time value of money is. Imagine Cruz's total had he continued to invest the entire time? Even if Zaya had continued investing beyond age 65, she would never catch up to Cruz. It doesn't matter if you read this book at age 12, 26, 39, 52, 71 or 89. The best time to start investing is NOW. Every single day you wait, you lose the impact from compounding interest – which Albert Einstein famously quoted as, "The 8th Wonder of the World". The impact on the future value of your account realized from procrastination is massively undermined and painstakingly reduced.

Here's another observation. From a behavioral standpoint, it is highly likely that those who do not start NOW, will probably never start. There is never a good time to make the sacrifice of saving. There is no convenient time. It is far too easy to put things off until "later".

Let's investigate the cost of procrastination a little more deeply. If you are 20 years old and you want to raise $100,000 by age 65, assuming you can expect a 10% annual return, you need only invest $1,372 today.

However, if you were a 50-year-old you would need to invest nearly $24,000 to obtain the same $100,000.

This is the cost of procrastination.

**It's not money that makes you financially successful, it's time.**

**Landmine Number Two:** Spending habits.

Here is another example where the problem is not the current president or low interest rates, it is us and our behavior. Our spending habits have a huge impact on our ability to accomplish our financial dreams and goals. To help understand this more deeply, let's examine a couple living a very typical American lifestyle.

Our married couple has a combined income of $60,000, which represents the annual average income in U.S. today. They don't spend extravagantly, and like many couples, they are concerned that they can't seem to save enough money. In my practice, we frequently meet many people in this same boat all of the time.

> *"We are not really spending a lot of money, but we just can't seem to find anywhere to save money becausewe're just not making enough!*

This same couple drives around in a $45,000 SUV with a Starbucks' latte in the cup holder and a brand-new iPhone. This is an example of how spending habits absolutely impact our ability to save more far more than even outside factors such as Wall Street and the stock market.

Let's put this in perspective. Let's say that while this same couple is on their way to work, each of them stops to get a cup of coffee and a pastry. It's reasonable to say that is a cost of $4.50. Later while at work, each of them grabs a soda from the vending machine for another 75 cents. Adding up their spending, they now have a combined daily spending of $10.50. Ask yourself this: are they doing anything outrageous? The answer is, "no".

In fact, our example is conservative on the cost of coffee, snacks, and vending machine items within today's pricing world. The actual totals are likely greater, but let's give this couple the benefit of the doubt. Even with that pricing generosity, if you assume that there are 22 working days per month, our couple is spending $231 each month, or $2,772 a year on extras—these expenditures aren't really even a meal. Plus, before they even see their earned money in their accounts the state and federal governments have taxed their wages. Assuming that they fall into the 30% combined tax bracket - they must earn more than $4,000 per year just to net enough money to waste away on frivolous things that aren't even improving their lives. Remember, they believe they cannot save any money....Hmmm.

Oddly enough, if our couple—let's call them the Johnson's—made one small change in stopping their daily snacking/coffee habit they could SAVE 5% of their income. It's true! They are literally spending more than 5% of their annual income on complete junk, stuff that they don't even need. They're piddling it away on nothing. The crazy thing is if ALL they did was save that 5% over 40 years, they would have earned more than one million dollars.

By choosing to save that 5% from the age of 20, earning 10% a year on the invested income, they could retire at age 65 with more than $1 million. This is proof that it's all about our behavior and our spending habits; it is not really about our income potential.

**Landmine Number Three:** Inflation

Since 1926, inflation has averaged 3% per year according to the US Department of Labor.

To put that in perspective, our money must double over 23 ½ years to keep a consistent standard of living. Consider how much money you spend each year on everything: food, clothes, furniture, children's needs, transportation and housing, etc. Whatever that amount is, per month, you're going to need to double that amount of income in 23 ½ years, just to keep pace with the standard of living that you have right now. Imagine, if you are 50 years old, when you reach age 73 or 74, you're going to need twice as much income just to live the same lifestyle that you are right now assuming that period represents a normal inflationary time period. Think about it, for a 40-year-old, by the time they reach mid-80s, they are going to need four times as much money just to live the same lifestyle as they were when they were 40 years old. How does this impact us as investors?

You must take action to grow our money to be sure you can meet the needs.

**If you:**
- ☐ **Are not saving**
- ☐ **Are not receiving regular pay increases at work**

☐ **Do not have money invested in vehicles that will beat inflation**
☐ **Are not earning regular adequate rates of return on our investments**

**You are LOSING money**

In a low interest rate environment like you've seen since the financial collapse of 2008, often times, savers or "safe money" investors, have felt secure in the fact that they're not losing any money in bank accounts and short-term interest-bearing accounts. Unfortunately, their real rate of return, relative to inflation, is absolutely negative. Remember every 23-1/2 years, on average, you need to double your money just to create as much retirement income as you enjoyed in the past.

Here's a practical analogy: If you throw a frog in boiling water, it will jump out. But, if you put the same frog in lukewarm water, and slowly raise the temperature, what will happen? Our frog friend is lulled into comfort and just stays in there until he eventually dies. Inflation isn't something that hits you all at once. It is a gradual burn on our finances over a long period of time; you don't even notice that it's happening until it's too late.

**Landmine Number Four:** Taxes.

We are all united in our dislike of taxes. According to the tax foundation, sometime over the first couple of weeks of April is really your tax freedom day--meaning that every dollar that you earn in the first three-and-a-half months of the year goes to pay your taxes. Here's another way to put it, nearly one third of our time at work every day is spent simply to work to pay our taxes.

Besides federal tax, there is also state tax, local tax, capital gains tax, estate tax, sales tax, and property tax. We're getting hit from taxes all over the place. Sometimes we lose sight of the fact that it's not what you make but rather what you keep that actually matters.

Taxes are a natural part of our lives, yet the tax efficiency of your portfolio is critically important. We must pay our fair share (and who can really know what that amount is) but there ARE specific strategies surrounding taxes that can significantly impact our ability to retire and retire well. When applied correctly, these tax strategies of future planning and being proactive may have a bigger impact on our success and our financial freedom than even the underlying investment performance itself. Sadly, many people have failed to do proactive planning.

If you have a CPA or a tax preparer who has called out of the blue - middle of the summer – to tell you about some great ideas that may help save taxes then you have found a fantastic CPA, keep him or her. The truth is that most Americans think they're doing tax planning when in reality they are merely doing tax preparation.

Forward thinking proactive tax planning is really what's critical and vital. Reactive tax preparation is what most of us are doing and it's not helping us save every tax dollar possible – a huge landmine, when it comes to our success as investors.

*Excerpts from Ric Edelman, The Truth About Money – 4th Edition Pages 48-66*

## Chapter #2 – End of Chapter Questions

Which 2 obstacles have impacted you most as an investor?

_____

_____

_____

_____

How So?

_____

_____

_____

_____

# Chapter Three:
# All Advisers are Not Actually Advisers

What if I told you that not every financial professional, even those who call themselves "financial advisers" are not, in fact, actually advisers?

Wondering what I mean? Not all advisers are created equal. There are many different types of financial professionals, from insurance agents to stock brokers, to bond brokers, to registered representatives, to financial advisers, to fiduciaries, and so on and so forth. In fact, it's pretty darn confusing. It is easy to see how Main Street Americans have difficulty understanding the difference or even knowing there IS a difference. My goal in this chapter is to help you understand the different types of advisers and how they differ from one another.

**The Registered Representative:** The traditional financial professional often called "adviser" is, actually, not a financial adviser at all, but rather a salesman. This individual represents a company and offers, sells, and solicits various investment vehicles in exchange for commission compensation from their broker-dealer and 3rd party companies. One of the easiest ways to distinguish this person is to look at the business card of the financial professional.

If you see language at the bottom of the card that says: Registered Representative of So-and-So Company (put any of the broker-dealers in there) this means this person represents the broker-dealer to solicit and sell various investment products on its behalf for commissions. These investment companies pay the representative compensation for placing your dollars with them. Many think they are going to a "financial adviser" because this is what they call themselves. Unfortunately, you are more aptly put, seeing an "investment salesperson".

*What's the problem with this?* Many of these types of financial professionals are not independent. This means the broker-dealer they work with has proprietary and incentivized products. These products offer the salesperson additional compensation in the form of bonuses or higher compensation percentage amounts when the sales person solicits and sells those specific vehicles. In short, as a hardworking Main Street American going to one of these "financial advisers"- AKA salesperson on behalf of their broker-dealer—you could be advised to purchase an investment vehicle primarily because it pays that salesperson considerably more money - even if it is NOT the very best vehicle for your given situation.

Unfortunately, because of this scenario, you are often offered strategies that may be reasonably suitable for you but are NOT promoting your best interest, nor the absolute best use of your dollars. In fact, there may even be some lower cost investments or better performing investments available. If these investments ARE NOT on the broker-dealers' wish list, likely because there are not compensation and revenue sharing agreements tied to them, you will likely not be offered these.

Sadly, you will lose as an investor because you're working with a registered representative who is burdened with conflicts of interest, and more specifically the interests of his company first, rather than yours.

The Insurance Agent: A second type of professional known as an adviser is the insurance agent. Most financial professions are also insurance agents. However, in some cases, you will be working with someone who is strictly an insurance agent. When you visit an insurance agent, do you think the advice you are given will ever be anything but "safe money" options? Probably not. The way these folks feed their families and pay their bills is by selling you insurance products. The agent whose livelihood is linked to selling insurance products--whether it be as an insurance agent or an insurance agent masquerading as a registered rep—you can bet your bottom dollar that their solution, regardless of your specific situation will be rooted in a massive amount of insurance products.

A more impactful dynamic of destruction is that you will never really know whether what they are offering is in your best interests or not, because if they don't sell one of their proprietary products - or they don't sell an insurance vehicle, they don't make any money. Their objective is to sell more products on behalf of their broker-dealer or insurance company rather than offering what is the absolute best for your situation and your hard-earned dollars. This makes it impossible for them to provide objective advice.

I believe the best adviser works hardest for whomever is paying him or her.

Wouldn't you agree with that? In other words, if your adviser is being paid by mutual fund companies and through bonuses from their broker-dealer, they are really working for THEM, not you. Although you may think you are going to meet with "YOUR financial adviser" you are actually seeing a salesman who is acting on behalf of and is responsible to a broker-dealer, or insurance company, not you as an investor.

**The Fee-Based Fiduciary:** The TRUE adviser is someone who offers you guidance and advice in exchange for a fee. My practice, Keystone Wealth Partners, is built on this principle. Whether anyone chooses me and my firm, or another quality firm in our area, they ought to be working with a fee-based, independent, registered investment advisory firm that has highly credentialed advisers. One of the differences is how we are paid. A set fee levied regardless of what types of investments are recommended compensates the true advisers, like Keystone Wealth Partners.

How does this payment structure benefit you? The professional whose fee is linked to accounts, has no financial incentive to advise you on anything that is not in your best interest. Why? You and the fee-based firm are on the same side of the table at that point. Everyone is on the same team. There are no payments being triggered by transactions. There are no commissions to the adviser through the selling of investment products. Instead, a fee is paid on an ongoing basis as long as you are satisfied and happy as a client. That's it. All recommendations are going to be in your best interests because they are also in the best interest of the adviser whose fee depends on the investments being efficiently managed.

Finally, it is important to find someone who operates under a fiduciary standard of care rather than a suitability standard. The registered representative outlined before, or the insurance agent, operate under a suitability standard of care, which means they're shockingly allowed to sell things that aren't actually the best strategies for you. Say what!? Yes, it's true. The only requirement is that they be suitable and reasonable. Fiduciaries are held to similar laws governing the CPA or the attorney.

The fiduciary operating as a financial adviser is required by law to put the best interests of the INVESTOR ahead of their own best interests. Furthermore, they also disclose in writing any conflicts of interest that may arise along the way.

Why would you even considering hiring an adviser who is NOT legally required to put your best interests ahead of their own? I have no idea? Maybe it's due to a lack of distinction? Shouldn't that be a given – that the advisers put the investor's interests ahead of their own and recommend only what is in your best interest? Unfortunately, the majority of financial advisers in existence today are not independent, fee-only fiduciaries. This is the only type of financial adviser I would recommend to someone who cares deeply about ensuring they receive objective advice.

The last characteristic you should expect in your financial adviser is that they are highly "credentialed." Someone can pass a simple 3-week test, print business cards, and hold themselves out as a financial adviser. They then walk their local neighborhood, knocking on doors, or make a list of 500 friends and family members to whom they are going to solicit their services.

The state advisory and insurance tests are not difficult to pass, and pass quickly. They also provide little practical knowledge to help the financial professional provide useful advice.

Would you allow an inexperienced individual who did not attend medical school perform open-heart surgery on you? Of course not, you would search high and low for one of the best cardiologists in your area. Regarding your life's savings, I believe you should take the same approach.

Here are the credentials I would look for. In my opinion, an adviser should possess one of these designations or degrees:
1. CFP®
2. ChFC®
3. MSFS or another Master's Degree within finance
4. PhD in economics, finance, etc.

So, let's recap the 4 required characteristics for hiring -- or continue working with -- a financial adviser:

1. Independent

2. Fee-Only

3. Fiduciary

4. Credentialed

Even if you follow this advice, a positive, long-term relationship of success is never guaranteed. However, at least it gives you the best foundation with which to work and move forward. Choosing an independent, fee-only fiduciary that is credentialed sets you up to achieve your goals because it aligns your adviser -- a true industry expert – with your interests, plain and simple.

## Chapter #3 – End of Chapter Questions

Do you know what your all-in cost is on your portfolio and your investments?

_____

_____

_____

_____

_____

_____

_____

_____

Do you know who pays your financial adviser and how much they're paid? (Is it investment companies, is it mutual fund companies, is it bonuses from their broker dealer, or are you writing them a direct payment?)

_____

_____

_____

_____

_____

_____

_____

_____

# Chapter Four:
# Annuities are Good, Bad and Ugly

Annuities. The very word itself stirs emotion within a lot of investors. There are so many opinions, so many different types, and so much misunderstanding surrounding them. To muddy the waters even more, insurance salesmen have abused the sales process and created tremendous confusion.

☐ **Should you own one?**
☐ **Is it the best retirement vehicle ever?**
☐ **Is it the worst retirement vehicle ever?**
☐ **Is it somewhere in between?**
☐ **Does it fit everyone's situation or only certain situations?**

To understand annuities, let's first examine the basic components and various types. There are three primary annuity categories, and it's important that I unpack each one briefly.

**The first is an immediate annuity.** Often referred to as a SPIA, this annuity is a single-premium immediate annuity. When most people hear the word "annuity," this is the type they associate with. It's the original annuity; a pension so-to-speak. In the days where most companies offered their retired employees pensions, there wasn't a huge appetite for immediate annuities.

However, today, defined benefit plans have mostly gone away in favor of defined contributions plans, such as 401(k)s, 457s, 403(b)s, etc. Because of this you now have the responsibility of generating your own retirement income. This income must last for the rest of your life, and you rarely have company pensions to rely on for that steady income. An immediate annuity is very similar to a typical company pension.

With an immediate annuity, at retirement time, you may take a lump sum of money and hand it over to an insurance company in exchange for a lifetime income benefit or possibly a lifetime income stream, just like a prototypical pension. There are various different types you can choose: 10-year plus periods, the remainder of your life, and many in between. If you choose the remainder of your life and you predecease your spouse, your spouse may get 50% or 100% depending on what you select at inception. All of these various options, combined with your life expectancy, impact the amount of the monthly check they provide in exchange for the lump sum you used to purchase the annuity.

**Here are the pros to this option.** These mirror the benefits from social security or a pension, although they are only as sound as the company insuring it.

1. **It's relatively secure.**
2. **It is cash that is sent on a regular basis.**
3. **It is not affected by the stock prices or the stock market volatility.**
4. **It creates predictability for your retirement income.**

**Here are the cons to this option.** First, there are those folks who choose a life-only option annuity and don't live very long unfortunately. The lump sum was exchanged for a lifetime income benefit or pension-type payments. This means these people who pass unexpectedly, soon after purchasing the annuity will not collect anywhere near the amount they used to purchase the annuity. Also, many SPIAs have no death benefit tied to them, which means the heirs will collect nothing at death. The money is gone.

The other negative is the fact that when you turn over that lump sum, you are sacrificing liquidity and flexibility. Should an unexpected medical expense occur, or you learn you must invest in a new roof for your home the lump sum is no longer available. When you choose this annuity, you must be certain to have access to other funds for emergencies. Many people mistakenly invest too high of a percentage of their liquid assets within a SPIA and find that later, although they have a guaranteed income stream, they do not have a cushion to help cover unexpected expenses.

**The second type of an annuity is a variable annuity.** Variable annuities are, by far, the largest segment of the annuity world at the present time. They are a securities product and an investment. A variable annuity comprises of what are called sub accounts. A sub account looks and feels similar to a mutual fund and is engineered by many of the same manufacturers.

Practically you can think of these as mutual funds – but keep in mind they are slightly different and are thus called "sub accounts" within a VA (variable annuity).

Your investment in these quasi mutual funds will rise and fall as their various holdings perform. They are no different than the other "market driven" investment vehicles you own from this perspective.

The sub accounts may consist of choices within large cap growth, small cap growth, international and emerging markets, bonds and all sorts of other asset classes. The price of these investments within the variable annuity fluctuate at the close of market each day, just as any other mutual fund account would do. As the market ceases trading for the day, they re-price. *With variable annuities, you must remember that your principal is not insured and will rise and fall with market fluctuations.*

What then makes it a variable annuity rather than just a group of poser mutual funds? Here is where the "annuity component" comes into play. These sub accounts are then wrapped into an insurance product - called a variable annuity - it may provide certain systematic income guarantees, along with possible enhanced death benefits as well.

The first way to trigger the "annuity strategy" with a VA is to annuitize the vehicle for a lifetime pension – converting it to something similar to the immediate annuity. In general, one of the features of these is that you can typically annuitize them at any point along the way, which allows you to convert your own into what looks, eats, and breathes like an immediate annuity.

Many variable annuities also offer what's called a guaranteed minimum income benefit, a GMIB benefit. Others offer a GWB, a guaranteed withdrawal benefit option. These benefit options are able to create some predictable form of withdrawal from your lump sum.

Even if the market and your underlying sub accounts drop in value and you live a long time, you may have an option to initiate one of those benefits and begin systematic income payments that continue even if your contract value drops to zero due to market volatility and the aforementioned withdrawals. Naturally, this is based upon the ability of the insurance company to pay claims, but assuming they can, you can continue to receive income.

Some variable annuities also contain a guaranteed enhanced death benefit, which has guaranteed components to the attached death benefit. To get this right, you must look at the specific annuities themselves.

**Here's the pros to a variable annuity:** you get to maintain the lump sum on your balance sheet, by comparison to the SPIA, where you have to give up the lump sum. You may also achieve market growth based upon the sub account performance. Lastly, your specific contract might also provide a guaranteed income benefit that would allow for lifetime income payments regardless of whether poor sub account performance runs the account balance to zero. Sounds like the best retirement vehicle on earth, right? Maybe.

**Here's the cons to a variable annuity:** Your principal is not insured or protected. Your sub accounts - the amount you can actually withdraw in a lump sum - are based on whatever the underlying investments' values are at the close of market on any given day. Like any other security, it is subject to market risk and short-term volatility. One of the other negatives to variable annuities is that they are one of the most expensive vehicles or products available.

If you add a guaranteed minimum income benefit and an enhanced death benefit on top of M & E fees, administrative fees, sub-account fees, etc; you are typically agreeing to pay upwards of 4% per year to the insurance company.

**These are internal fees, so you never see them.**

They're not a line-item on your statement.

These fees are something you are absolutely paying, and they are consistently eating away at your account value. And at 4%, they are taking a large bite!

**The third type of annuity is a fixed annuity.** These operate quite differently than either of the other two. A fixed annuity is a vehicle that provides principal-insurance, and is protected against market losses based upon the claims paying ability of the insurance company.

This means if you put $100,000 into a fixed annuity, it's protected and insured. It operates similar to a CD, although obviously a CD is FDIC insured, and an insurance company insures a fixed annuity. Your money in a fixed annuity is not subjected to market risk. In exchange for your investment, the insurance company provides you with an interest rate much like any other type of CD or interest-bearing account. Typically, the rates are higher than a CD because they're not FDIC insured.

There is another vehicle that is a type of spinoff within the fixed annuity family that has grown in popularity over the past couple decades. It's called a fixed indexed annuity. These maintain the same characteristics of a fixed annuity, in that your principal is protected against market losses.

However, instead of taking a set, predetermined interest rate - especially in a low interest rate environment like today - you are able to link your returns to a specific index such as the S&P500. Then, based on an annual performance of the specified index, you receive a portion of that growth as your interest rate for the year. Conversely, if that index goes down in value, you lose nothing. When it increases, you receive an increase.

Here is an example to help conceptualize indexed annuities: A fixed indexed annuity may provide approximately 50% of whatever the S&P 500 does during each contract year. In this investment, you receive 50% of the growth with no market downside. It locks in the credited interest every year. Index dividends are not included in this product; it's only the index itself. If the index goes up 10%, you would earn 5% in this example. Let's suppose you had $100,000 invested, your account would earn $5,000, and grow to $105,000. That growth locks in and now represents your new insured value. Your account can't drop below $105,000 regardless of market performance in future contract years. There is some potential for growth, while your principal remains insured against losses. When you allocate $100,000 to an indexed annuity you know that it's secured from ever dipping below $100,000 due to market losses.

These fixed annuities are also called equity-indexed annuities. The most obvious pro to this annuity is that your principal is insured so you don't have market risk. You can't lose money as long as the insurance company remains solvent. The fees – if there are any – are significantly lower than a variable annuity.

It is still possible to attach lifetime income guarantees, such as guaranteed withdrawal benefits and/or enhanced death benefits to these, just as you can with variable annuities to assure the guaranteed lifetime income if desired.

The primary negative attribute to fixed annuities, just as with any deferred annuity, is that you do not have immediate liquidity for all of the money.

Typically, these equity-indexed annuities are offered in 7, 10, 12, or 15-year contracts. With most annuities it is possible to take 10% out in any given year after year one, penalty-free. Part of the reason you may enjoy great benefits from a fixed annuity is because you agree to keep some of the money at the insurance company for several years. Once again, this negative aspect of foregoing full and immediate access to your money is one you must be mindful of and agree to.

It is vital that any annuity is utilized within the context of an individualized, customized, personalized financial plan to ensure that your cash flow and other liquidity sources are adequate enough to handle any unexpected expenses that could arise.

Sometimes those nearing retirement like the benefits of a fixed annuity. Decent growth, with no market risk. Sign me up! However, it sounds great only until people put too much of their nest egg into it – often because they're simply terrified of market volatility and like the idea of having their money insured. You must be very, very careful with annuities. Be extremely mindful not to act on any of the subjects in this book – especially annuities - without fully reading all the disclosures and gaining advice from a knowledgeable financial adviser.

As a Certified Annuity Specialist (CAS®), I recommend speaking to someone who is a Certified Annuity Specialist before making any type of decision related to an annuity. There are thousands of specific annuities, and hundreds of insurance companies out there, and you must be vigilant prior to implementing any annuities.

Because annuities have limited liquidity, you must ensure your entire financial situation has been considered prior to purchasing one.

**Chapter Disclosure:** There are thousands of different types of annuities available. Each state has specific rules regarding which annuities, and which annuity companies are approved to operate within that state. This chapter's concise explanation is intended for educational purposes. Decisions to invest in these types of annuities should begin with viewing the prospectus and then with consulting a financial adviser.

# Chapter #4 – End of Chapter Questions

### *Annuities are Good, Bad and Ugly*

Do you know if an annuity should be an item in your retirement toolbox, and if so which type of annuity--immediate, variable, or fixed?

_____

_____

_____

_____

_____

# Chapter Five:
# The Mortgage Trick

One of the most destructive things for American homeowners has been the inability to understand one simple truth over the last nine decades. You've been taught for years that minimizing debt and deleveraging is the financially responsible thing to do – all the time. In most cases it is. In fact, it is almost always better to get out of debt rather than shell out interest payments.

There's one caveat, one primary exception to this rule and that is paying off a home early by making extra mortgage payments or paying cash for a primary residence. Why would this be a mistake? There are several reasons why but before we unpack them lets track this back to its origin and examine why many people believe this myth to be true.

This belief dates back to the 1920s. Our parents taught us to pay off our house early, and their parents taught them to pay off their house early, and their parents taught them to do the same. In the 1920s, paying off a home early made perfect sense because many mortgages were only offered for five-year terms. These mortgages were known as callable loans— the bank was able to call the loan at any time, and if the family could not come up with the balance, the family would be displaced. They would be forced to move. Even in the fortunate scenario where the loan wasn't called, they would hope and pray that they could refinance or re-qualify for another loan in order to stay after the initial 5-year term ended.

The only way to create true peace of mind was to do whatever you could to pay off your house early - and as quickly as possible. A tremendous amount of families were impacted during the years following the 1920s when the Great Depression hit in the 1930s.

It's easy to see why this fear and experience has led to decades of misinformation regarding paying off mortgages early. Mortgage reform occurred in the years following the depression, adjusting house notes to 30-year mortgages as they are still offered today.

**Let's look at a few of the reasons why you may want to consider NOT paying off your mortgage early.**

When you sign for a $500,000 mortgage you see in black and white the amount of interest you will pay if not paid off early. That interest amount could be close to $750,000 - on top of the $500,000 principal. You might think "Why wouldn't I want to make extra payments to my house so that I do not have to pay $1,250,000 for a $500,000 home?"

The first reason is that mortgages are cheap money. To be clear, mortgages are the cheapest money you will ever be able to borrow. Don't believe me, where else can you borrow several hundred thousand dollars over 30 years for less than 5% interest? Because the bank uses the home itself as collateral if you are unable to pay the money back – and they expect the home value to grow over time – they offer you a very low interest rate. The more confident they are in your ability to pay them back based upon credit score, assets, liabilities, and a variety of other factors the lower the rate. By contrast credit cards are the opposite, and thus double-digit interest rates that sometimes climb as high as 30% per year. Having a mortgage creates potential leverage to build wealth quicker.

The second reason for not paying cash for your house is liquidity. The moment your money is applied to the home, liquidity is lost without any real possibility of getting it out, aside from borrowing it from the bank. Things could change in your life, and you could need access to that cash. What if you are unable to use the equity you have built up? What if present interest rates preclude you from practically doing so? Had you saved your money in an interest-bearing account, you would have access to it at any time. Imagine, you could lose your job, have a medical emergency - whatever occurs - you would be able to use your own money when you needed it if you didn't sink it into your home.

The third principal regards the rate of return on equity. Most people completely misunderstand this concept. They mistakenly compare the appreciation of a home with the rate of return on the equity inside the home.

Think of this example: Two neighbors buy $500,000 houses, one neighbor pays cash for his house and the other neighbor puts down 20% - $100,000 - and finances the other 400,000 over 30-years. Two years later there's an oil boom in the neighborhood and both houses appreciate to $1 million dollars. Did either house grow more than the other because of the mortgage balance, or lack of mortgage balance? No.

Assuming both homes are the same floor plan with similar values, both houses grew in value by $500,000. Each home appreciated $500,000. Whether you financed or paid cash in full, both homes appreciated by the exact same amount.

The appreciation of the homes is not linked in any way to the amount of equity realized in your home. In fact, one could argue that the person who put only $100,000 down made $500,000 on their $100,000 investment. This means the cash on cash return was five times principal, or 500%. The other person invested the full amount - $500,000 - and earned only a 100% rate of return on their money.

Ultimately, neither of them truly received any rate of return on their money but rather asset appreciation due to home prices rising. However, let's view the situation in terms of how much of their own cash each had to outlay. One used $100,000 and the other used the full $500,000 for the same amount of appreciation. Wouldn't you choose to use the least amount of money possible to get the exact same amount of appreciation?

**In fact, did you know the rate of return on your equity is guaranteed to be zero?**

That's right, it is 0%. This means the second your money is invested into the bricks and mortar of your home it will earn a 0% rate of return forever. In reality, it actually loses an average of more than 3% a year due to inflation. Can you imagine putting your money into any investment that was guaranteed to earn 0% forever? Although the home will likely appreciate over time, that will occur independently of any equity requirements on your part. You enjoy the appreciation regardless.

The icing on the cake is that mortgage payments get easier over time. When my parents bought my childhood home on 222nd street in Kent, Washington they paid less than $90,000. Their monthly mortgage payment at that time was approximately $500 per month. How in the world would they afford such an expensive monthly payment? As a result of inflation, does a $500 mortgage now seem expensive? Of course not! Historically speaking, every 20-25 years your mortgage payment effectively is half what is was at loan inception.

Here is a great side note: even if 10-years into your 30-year mortgage, you decide that you would prefer to pay off your mortgage, you can drive down to the bank and pay off your mortgage early with no penalties. You maintain full control at all times, even if you change your mind.

This philosophy holds up in any interest rate environment but consider how effective this is with today's historically low interest rates. You are able lock in a low rate for 30-years, then invest the extra dollars in the future at assumed higher rates. This allows you to borrow LOW and earn higher returns by leveraging that money in compounding interest vehicles once rates rise.

Since the majority of you own a home, this is one of the most important principals for you to understand and take advantage of. Unfortunately, a lack of sound guidance surrounding home mortgages has cost many Americans millions of dollars that could have otherwise been used to fund retirement accounts and enhance their legacies.

## Chapter #5 – End of Chapter Questions

Do you currently have a mortgage?

_____

_____

_____

_____

_____

If not, why??

_____

_____

_____

_____

_____

# Chapter Six:
# Wear Gold,
# Don't Invest in it

Gold is an investment that is often sold, and rarely bought.

Here's what I mean, few people wake up and say to themselves, "Today is the day I am going to go and invest in gold." Instead, aggressive gold salespeople using fear and scare tactics SELL gold. When people buy gold, there are typically several steps behind the sale. They must be skilled salespeople because they manage to sell a commodity that possesses little historical evidence or data that would support it as a good investment. Despite the facts, gold continues to be solicited and purchased by many American investors.

**What are the reasons someone might consider investing in gold?**

Potential growth is one of the first objectives some seek when they buy gold within their portfolio. However, the high volatility when compared to its historical long-term growth provides no evidence supporting the suitability of owning gold for anything more than speculative purposes. In fact, a few decades ago, gold hit an all-time high on the New York Mercantile Exchange and was trading at $850 an ounce.

It then proceeded to drop in value for the next 235 months. After its tumble, gold took 28 years to recover its value back to its high of $850.

*Can you imagine owning any investment, whether it be real estate, a diversified stock port/olio, or bonds, where 25 years into the investment holding period you were still down in value?*

This is exactly what happened with gold.

Since 1927, gold's average rate of return has been just over 3.5% per year while the stock market has been over 10%.

In the end, the level of volatility and standard deviation that gold provides relative to its ability to grow is atrocious when compared to other investment options.

An effective inflation hedge is the second reason that many people consider gold as an investment. During times of expected high inflation, many believe buying gold will offer a strong hedge against it. Remember President Jimmy Carter? From 1979 to 1983, America had some of its highest levels of inflation in United States history when it topped out at 7% per year. Yet, gold barely kept up with HALF the pace of inflation - not a good example supporting gold as a sound tool to battle inflation.

The third reason that people buy gold is because they react to the world's fear mongers who are wringing their hands circulating the notion that the world is ending and that gold will be the only safe means of currency. This may sound ridiculous, but there are people who believe this to be true.

Sadly, the gold salesmen leverage these fears and prey on those folks by offering gold as the only "safe alternative" to paper currency and investments that will be "worthless".

Here's the problem with this theory:

If you look at gold's movement relative to the US dollar, nearly 80% of the time over the last 40-years gold has moved in tandem with the US Dollar.

In other words, when the dollar weakens, 80 percent of the time, gold is moving in the same direction. To sum it up, gold is not a suitable non-correlated asset class to the devaluing dollar.

Another item that gold has working against it is that gold does not possess an ability to compound its growth. The compound interest that you receive in a diversified stock portfolio is never achieved when investing in gold. In equities, you have the benefit of compound interest based upon the profitability and growth of the companies you own. As a part owner, you own an equity stake as a stockholder.

With gold bars, unless they figure out a way to procreate inside of your safe at home, or inside of the storage facility of the gold investment house, it doesn't increase in value unless the underlying price of gold rises - there is no compound effect. When you open your safe, the five gold bars you placed in there ten years before are still five gold bars; in the stock market, you benefit from the compound interest and possible reinvestment of those profits.

I have to be direct here: gold sucks. You should wear it, buy it for those that you love as jewelry, but avoid this speculative commodity as an investment of your life's savings.

## Chapter #6—End of Chapter Questions

Do you currently own gold?_____Yes    _____No

What compelled you to buy it originally?

_____

_____

_____

_____

_____

_____

_____

Who originally told you that it was a good idea to buy it?

_____

_____

_____

_____

_____

# Chapter Seven:
# Keeping it, Not Making it Is
# WHAT MATTERS

When it comes to investments, many focus on investment returns. They spend tremendous amounts of time trying to figure out what investments to purchase, how long to hold them, whether to stay in them, sell them, and whether to buy this investment or that investment. What should the asset allocation be for your mix of stocks and bonds? The energy and effort spent engineering fundamentally sound investment portfolios may lead to increased accumulation, but unfortunately it is often wasted due to a lack of forward-thinking tax planning. Unfortunately, even those who are the most disciplined savers and investors may not realize their full monetary potential, because success is not found only in what you make, but rather what you keep.

There is an insidious little thing called taxes. You are probably aware that you are responsible to pay taxes each year, and the more you earn, the greater your tax bill typically is. As a Certified Tax Specialist, one of the areas that my colleagues and I at Keystone Wealth Partners emphasize with clients is how to minimize taxes not only in the current year, but also how to minimize total taxes over long periods of time.

Whether you are an accumulator trying to figure out how to save during your highest income-earning years, or you are retired and trying to figure out how to get distributions out of your IRA as tax-efficiently as possible, taxes have a huge impact on your legacy.

Tax strategies alone can fill hundreds of pages, and my purpose for this chapter is not to pour over each specific strategy. Too often, many believe that they are doing tax planning, but what they are actually doing is tax preparation. Let me explain: at the end of the year, you go to your CPA and ask them to put all the right numbers in the right boxes. Your CPA tells you your bill, you cut the check, and you're done.

The fact is, having someone reactively preparing your tax return, is not helping you make proactive planning changes. This is nothing more than tax filing. Tax planning means a professional analyzes your income numbers, your deductions, and reviews all available tools that could help you reduce your future tax bill. True, comprehensive tax planning involves forecasting 10, 20, 30, or even 40-years into the future. Sadly, very few have actually done this.

For most, the primary "proactive" tax-planning tool used is to defer as much income as possible through the use of a 401(k), IRA, etc. Before we accept this as the obvious solution for tax-minimization, let's examine it a bit more. There are only three possible outcomes regarding future tax rates. Tax rates may rise, stay the same, or fall. When taxes remain stable, it is a wash, when they fall you benefit from the savings of tax deferral.

However, when they rise, you will wish you had simply paid the taxes prior rather than pushing them out to a later, higher rate environment. In each scenario, tax planning allows you to fare better in the long run.

Although no one knows the future for certain, there are several reasons I believe taxes will increase in the future, and therefore deferring massive amounts of your net worth in tax-deferred retirement accounts, such as 401(k)s and IRAs, may be less than beneficial in the long run.

Did you know that nearly 75% of our entire federal budget pays for only 4 expense items: Social Security, Medicare, Medicaid, and interest on our national debt. If untouched, that 75% percentage will increase above 90% within the next 10 years

Due to the size of the "Baby Boomer" generation, combined with medical advancements that have Americans living longer than ever before, a once 40:1 ratio of Social Security contributors to participants has shrunk to 3:1. Suggesting taxes are going to increase doesn't require me to harness my psychic powers, but rather pull out a calculator. Simple math determines that to remain solvent, our federal government will be forced to increase taxes in the future. If this is the case, then why are the majority of assets saved for retirement done so in accounts that are kicking the tax-can down the curb?

Here are a few questions to start asking yourself as you begin your journey of forward thinking, proactive tax-planning:
- **Should you be deferring now?**
- **Should you be doing a Roth conversion?**

☐ **Should you be contributing to a Roth IRA or contributing to a normal Traditional IRA?**

☐ **Should you be splitting your 401(k) contributions between half Roth and half Traditional, if those are available for you?**

☐ **In retirement, should you be doing Roth conversions, accelerating required minimum distributions prior to 70-1/2, filling up brackets triggering long-term capital gains ahead of time within the 10% or 15% tax bracket?**

☐ **Are your heirs in higher or lower tax-brackets than you?**

☐ **If you plan to pass money to charities at death, what types of accounts are most tax-efficient to gift them?**

☐ **Will compound growth increase your net worth above the estate tax exemption?**

These are just a few of the things that need to be considered and oftentimes can make a huge difference on your overall success.

In terms of your legacy, the strategies applied and how you pass inherited money on to beneficiaries can have a massive impact on how much they get and how much the IRS receives. I assume that you would prefer the majority of your life savings and hard-earned assets go to charities that you care about and family members that you love, rather than the Internal Revenue Service. Unfortunately, some of you have structured a portfolio that neither reflects this nor includes an estate plan that will correctly implement these things.

Do you own dividend-oriented investments within your IRA or taxable account? Why not trigger dividends within an IRA where none of it is taxed until withdrawn?

This may allow you to be more tax efficient in seeking long-term growth within taxable accounts where higher turnover or dividends may create additional, and unwanted taxation. At death, your children receive a step up in cost basis from taxable accounts, and there you have it, you just disinherited the IRS from those hard-earned dollars.

If you desire money to go to charities and some to your family members, why not pass IRA assets onto 501c(3), which will be tax exempt and pass the non-qualified money to the children in order to get a step-up in basis so that they don't have to pay any tax either? Sorry IRS, nothing left for you to get your paws on!

There are several different strategies available that permit you to completely disinherit the IRS from your estate plan, yet so few people have actually had the guidance or the foresight to do so.

## Chapter #7—End of Chapter Questions

When is the last time you did forward-thinking tax?

Do you have a professional that performs this for you?

_____

_____

_____

How will social security benefits impact my overall tax responsibility?

_____

_____

_____

What tax bracket are my heirs in?

_____

_____

What tax bracket will I be in if my spouse pre-deceases me?

_____

_____

_Inspired by David McKnight, The Power of Zero_

# Chapter Eight:
# At the Market's Mercy

When people sit down to meet with us at Keystone Wealth Partners, they sometimes ask, "What returns can I expect you to make for me?" This question is of course nearly impossible to answer with certainty. Fortunately for those in retirement - who are taking distributions from their portfolio - it is <u>not</u> anywhere near the most important question.

You see, most of you were conditioned to believe that your financial success primarily hinged on achieving the highest average rate of return. While you were young and still working to accumulate wealth, this belief was true. Although this is still partially true, it's only entirely true while you are YOUNG.

When you reach retirement, the most important question changes dramatically. It's no longer only about how high the returns are, but rather where, and in what order will you capture those returns. The strategy that you deploy to control the predictability of returns becomes vital to retirement success.

To be clear, the sequence of your returns, in fact, has no impact while you are saving for retirement. However, once you retire and are required to take withdrawals from your accounts, the value of your investments <u>at the time of those withdrawals</u> becomes vital, particularly if you must withdraw significant amounts of money.

Avoiding selling investments while they are down in value is critical to having your money last for a lifetime.

Consider two 40-year olds who invest differently from one another as they attempt to accumulate money for retirement. Because each has deployed their own investment strategy, their accounts produce completely different orders of returns over the following 25-year period leading up to retirement. Although their sequences of returns varied, let's assume that they both averaged 8% per year when all was said and done. As you might suspect, each would have the exact same amount of money at the end of their accumulation periods - at age 65. How can that be since their "good" and "bad" years differed from one another?

The answer: Both investors earned the same rate of return on average over those 25 years. When they were saving money, the order didn't matter and had no impact on their final account values.

Both retirees and accumulators alike often struggle to understand this concept. Have you ever wondered why generally younger investors are told to have a higher portfolio percentage allocated into stocks? With longer time horizons prior to withdrawals, they need not worry about short-term volatility. Higher levels of volatility combined with a properly diversified portfolio will typically result in a higher average rate of return when compared historically to a less volatile portfolio. The final AVERAGE rate of return is all that matters when accumulating and not taking withdrawals. The orders of those returns are meaningless and thus investors who are far away from needing portfolio withdrawals should think only about achieving the highest average rate of return.

However, once money is needed to be withdrawn from the portfolio, the order – or sequence of returns - is one of the most important factors of your success. This happens to be a primary reason that a properly engineered financial plan becomes even more critical at retirement once retirement savings is needed for living expenses.

Remember our two investors? Let's fast-forward 25-years to their retirement dates and assume that they both continue to invest and receive different rates of return each year. Because they maintain different investment strategies, their accounts do not mirror one another.

Remember, they are now retired 65-year olds and need to begin withdrawing money to replace their lost wages. Each determined that they would need to withdraw 5% of their account value each year to support their retirement lifestyle.

Note: Each retiree believes that since they have earned 8% per year, on average, the past 25 years they should comfortably be able to withdraw 5% annually in retirement- and even make an extra 3% annually on top of it all. Both expect to leave huge legacies for their children and charities since their net worth will most certainly be growing by 3% per year, even while taking 5% of their lump sum in retirement distributions.

Not so much.

Imagine that each retiree is offered the chance to receive the same annual order of returns that the previous 25-years has produced for them (remember this was a sequence that averaged 8% per year). Both will most likely jump at that opportunity.

Neither will adjust their strategies to dampen volatility in retirement, because they are happily taking the 8% average rates of return they have grown accustomed to. However, this may not work out as well as they hope.

The first retiree receives the same sequence of returns at 65 that he received at age 40, 25-years earlier. Unfortunately, he will completely run out of money by age 82 – even though he averaged an 8% rate of return just as before and only needed to withdraw 5% per year.

How did this occur? This retiree faced large corrections as well as a bear market over the first 3-years of retirement. This required him to sell more shares at discounts during a depressed market to produce his needed retirement income stream. Even once the market rebounded in the 4th year of retirement, there no longer were not enough shares to sustain him over the remainder of his lifetime.

Think this scenario could never happen to you? This negative sequence of returns is the exact situation that many Americans faced who retired in 2000 or 2007, prior to the ".com" and "Credit Crisis" bear markets.

On the other hand, let's suppose the second retiree invested in different strategies and therefore received the opposite sequence of returns from our first retiree (meaning the aforementioned volatile correction and bear market happened at the conclusion of retirement instead of the beginning). As luck would have it, simply avoiding a down market early in retirement meant that this retiree had more in her account at age 90 than she began with at age 65, even while taking 5% withdrawals for the past 25 years!

Imagine these two retirees having a conversation at age 90 about their investment experiences. The first retiree, who is completely out of money, asks the second retiree, who has more money than ever, "What did you earn? What have you done? What did your adviser recommend? You must have had incredible investments!" Our second retiree shrugs her shoulders and says: "I think I've been making about 8% per year for the last 50 years."

The first retiree feels confused and dejected. After all, he thought he had been earning 8% per year for the last 50-years as well. How then could he have run out of money 8 years ago, while she has plenty of assets to leave a large inheritance to her heirs?

The ironic part of our example is that both in fact earned exactly an average 8% rate of return. However, when our first retiree left work, he lost tremendous amounts of money because of an unfortunate sequence of returns in those first few years.

Conversely, our second retiree benefitted from a nice bull market immediately after she retired. Even with the same average rate of return, a different sequence of returns can equate to a completely different legacy.

*It's not always HOW you invest, but also WHEN you invest.*

If you think the only factor in controlling your sequence of returns is your asset allocation, think again. When you choose to retire can be nearly as impactful, and how the market fares over those first 5 years may ultimately determine your destiny.

The following chart communicates this point perfectly.
Retiring in 1969 produced a higher average rate of return
than 1979, yet was ironically still a much worse year to
retire overall.

| Age | Mr. Smith Investment $100,000 Stocks 60% \| Bonds 40% Retired 1/1/1969 - Annual withdrawals $5,000 | | | Mrs. Jones Investment $100,000 Stocks 60% \| Bonds 40% Retired 1/1/1979 - Annual withdrawals $5,000 | | |
|---|---|---|---|---|---|---|
| | Year | ROR | Year-end Value | Year | ROR | Year-end Value |
| 65 | 1969 | -2.6% | $92,168 | 1979 | 14.7% | $109,172 |
| 66 | 1970 | 5.3% | $91,449 | 1980 | 23.9% | $128,899 |
| 67 | 1971 | 10.5% | $95,219 | 1981 | 3.4% | $126,282 |
| 68 | 1972 | 12.9% | $101,447 | 1982 | 16.6% | $139,848 |
| 69 | 1973 | -6.6% | $88,410 | 1983 | 16.6% | $155,426 |
| 70 | 1974 | -12.6% | $70,219 | 1984 | 7.3% | $158,880 |
| 71 | 1975 | 25.1% | $80,085 | 1985 | 22.0% | $185,630 |
| 72 | 1976 | 16.5% | $85,107 | 1986 | 13.9% | $203,223 |
| 73 | 1977 | -2.4% | $74,324 | 1987 | 5.7% | $206,232 |
| 74 | 1978 | 6.3% | $69,660 | 1988 | 12.2% | $222,537 |
| 75 | 1979 | 14.7% | $69,487 | 1989 | 22.1% | $262,402 |
| 76 | 1980 | 23.9% | $74,222 | 1990 | 1.2% | $255,753 |
| 77 | 1981 | 3.4% | $63,670 | 1991 | 20.8% | $298,808 |
| 78 | 1982 | 16.6% | $60,391 | 1992 | 6.1% | $306,574 |
| 79 | 1983 | 16.6% | $56,145 | 1993 | 7.3% | $318,026 |
| 80 | 1984 | 7.3% | $45,480 | 1994 | 2.0% | $313,351 |
| 81 | 1985 | 22.0% | $40,198 | 1995 | 24.6% | $378,884 |
| 82 | 1986 | 13.9% | $30,286 | 1996 | 16.3% | $429,072 |
| 83 | 1987 | 5.7% | $15,941 | 1997 | 21.1% | $507,502 |
| 84 | 1988 | 12.2% | $1,176 | 1998 | 19.1% | $592,094 |
| 85 | 1989 | 22.1% | Exhausted | 1999 | 14.3% | $664,249 |
| 86 | 1990 | 1.2% | Exhausted | 2000 | -0.8% | $645,969 |
| 87 | 1991 | 20.8% | Exhausted | 2001 | -3.8% | $608,120 |
| 88 | 1992 | 6.1% | Exhausted | 2002 | -9.3% | $538,413 |
| 89 | 1993 | 7.3% | Exhausted | 2003 | 18.9% | $626,319 |
| 90 | 1994 | 2.0% | Exhausted | 2004 | 8.2% | $663,790 |
| 91 | 1995 | 24.6% | Exhausted | 2005 | 3.8% | $674,761 |
| 92 | 1996 | 16.3% | Exhausted | 2006 | 11.2% | $735,149 |
| 93 | 1997 | 21.1% | Exhausted | 2007 | 6.1% | $764,278 |
| 94 | 1998 | 19.1% | Exhausted | 2008 | -20.5% | $591,402 |
| | Average ROR 10.5% | | | Average ROR 9.6% | | |

*(note: withdrawals increase with inflation annually)*

As you can see, your retirement strategy must take into account the unpredictability of year to year returns to ensure that when bear markets occur, you either have portions of your portfolio secure and insulated from downward market movement, or portions allocated to income-oriented investments that produce dividends unrelated to the current share price. Doing this allows the more volatile investments in your financial plan the necessary time to rebound and grow over long periods of time.

As you grow nearer to retirement, it is time to stop asking, "What's my rate of return?" Instead, the more important question is, "How do I engineer a well-defined income strategy that ensures I don't end up like "Mr. Smith."

In almost all cases, including stocks in your investment plan is prudent, but you must do so in coordination with safer, shorter-term investments that allow those growth-oriented stocks the necessary time to grow within the volatile context that they historically have.

It is also important that you work with an adviser who specializes in working with retirees and those nearing retirement age. Your adviser must intimately understand the nuances that unpredictable sequences of returns have on your retirement sustainability.

If your adviser's only strategy is to chase the highest average rate of return - or if you have been aiming for this on your own - you may achieve your goal, and sadly still run out of money.

## Chapter #8—End of Chapter Questions

If you are retired or nearing retirement, do you have a defined plan for beating this sequence of return risk?

_____

_____

_____

_____

_____

_____

# Chapter Nine:
# <u>Three Myths of Destruction</u>

Most of us have been taught three primary myths. And as investors you have also been influenced by the stories that Wall Street and the financial community wants you to hear. What you have been taught and what the truth is, are two very different things. My mission as an independent fiduciary is to set the record straight, to stop all the confusion and eliminate the perpetuation of these myths. Let's examine the three myths that have caused more financial destruction over the last 50-years than any others.

**The first myth is stock picking.** Stock selection is when you choose individual stocks because you hope (and believe) that they will grow in value so that you can make more money. The lie is that there are likely consistent and predictable values added through handpicking individual stocks.

There are two different ways to execute this. The first is obvious. You go out, or you direct your stockbroker to go out and purchase individual stocks based upon what you think is going to happen with that specific company. You research data, you research earning reports, and you try to figure out if you should purchase the stock or not. You buy it and then you agonize over whether you should sell the stock. Hold it? Sell it?

Stockbrokers have tried to demonstrate that they can do this. However, there is no academic evidence of anyone ever being able to do this consistently or predictably over long periods of time. Sure, you can buy a stock, hit on it, and see growth. I'm not denying that on occasion, you may have owned stocks that you feel have done pretty well for you. Most stocks over time will, in fact, grow because the stock market - as a whole — grows over time as well. If you have tried to do this for any extended period of time you almost certainly recognize that you will have some winners and some losers. It is virtually impossible that any amount of research can be done that will allow you to select the "correct" stocks consistently and predictably. The financial industry has done a masterful job of disguising this unpredictability through thousands mutual funds.

**Mutual funds.** You may agree, and concede that you cannot choose the right stocks at the right time. You've probably also learned through experience that your stock broker cannot distinguish the best stocks ahead of time either. However, many of you believe – at least inadvertently by your investment holdings - that professional money managers in charge of managing active mutual funds do in fact have an ability to do this.

Nothing could be further from the truth. In fact, if you purchased the average United States stock mutual fund 40-years ago, and you got the mean performance, $100,000 would have grown to approximately $2.4 million dollars. Let's pause for a moment to examine this. If you invested $100,000 with your broker, who in turn sold you a variety of mutual funds that were now worth nearly $2.5M dollars 40-years later you would most likely be pretty happy with the results.

You might even ask them for more business cards so that you can hand them out to all of your friends. After all your broker found you the best mutual fund managers, and helped you make a ton of dough over the past 4 decades.

You're probably thinking that the mutual funds you bought were well worth the commission you paid since those money managers obviously knew which stocks to buy.

Note: Inside of an equity mutual fund that is precisely what is happening – stock picking. You are paying fees – typically, high fees – under the premise that this "guru" has an expertise to buy and sell the right stocks, at the right time.

Since your $100,000 grew to $2.4 million, you probably would have thought that they did just that. Sadly, what really happened had little or nothing to do with expert stock-picking. Had you invested in a much lower cost ETF or Index Fund that simply bought and held the 500 largest U.S. stocks, your $100,000 would have grown to $4.7 million, nearly DOUBLE what you earned from the average U.S. active mutual fund investment during that same span.

That is the truth. You would have earned a full $2 million more had you abandoned trying to hire money managers who deceive you into thinking that they can pick all the stocks at the right time when they are, in fact, charging high expense ratios and commissions to under-perform.

*Not only do they not make you more money; they've lost you – and millions of other unsuspecting Americans -tremendous amounts of money over the years.*

**The second myth is track record investing.** Track record investing is defined as any circumstance where performance history is used to draw conclusions for what the best future investments will. Hopefully by now you acknowledge that the "average" stock picker - even professional money manager - gets crushed regularly by the market.

However, what if you are able to find a "better than average" mutual fund ahead of time? Although the average manager is unable pick the right investments, the "best of the best" might be able to, right? If only you could find the best investments ahead of time, then you could achieve fanatic results.

Here is the issue with that theory: There is no way to accomplish that. The only logical data-point is to study past performance. Have you ever looked at the star rating on Morningstar to help you pick a mutual fund? If you have, you're not alone. Have you ever analyzed the past performance of your 401(k) fund options to help you choose which one to invest in?

What if I told you that there's little to no correlation between past performance and future performance? Sure, you have most likely seen this specific disclosure language on an investment prospectus, but since you don't know the future, the past is the only thing to base your decision off of, right?

You may have even been advised at some point to get out of your current mutual funds in favor of one that has been performing better. This sounds logical, but is there any academic basis for such a decision? The truth is that this is only relevant if positive past performance is a viable indicator for the future.

Unfortunately for track record investors, it is not. In fact, approximately 85% of all active mutual funds will lose to their broad asset class in any given year. 8.5 out of 10 mutual fund managers will under-perform their comparable benchmark by attempting to handpick individual stocks. It's a loser's game.

There is one more thing that's important for you to know. With an approximate 30,000 mutual funds in existence, even though 25,500 will typically lose to their benchmarks, it still leaves 4,500 managers in any given year that will over-perform their comparable broad asset category. Make no mistake, when you go to a traditional financial adviser or broker, they will undoubtedly offer to sell you one of those 4,500 that recently performed well. Without understanding the "law of large numbers" – it's a mathematical certainty that some will over-perform based upon sheer volume of total funds - you might be tricked in the moment to believing that these "winners" are the best places to invest. Sadly, many will apply this false premise only to determine that over the decade, 85% of those funds will also lose to their broad asset categories on average.

You may get lucky here and there, but track record investing is no way to invest with any sort of peace of mind or confidence over long periods of time. The next time you see a magazine cover proclaiming "this guru" or "that guru" as the next great money manager, keep in mind that there will always be someone who got emerges a winner. The next time you spot a headline stating, "How these Wall Street Titans outperformed the markets", keep in mind that it's purely mathematical.

The certainty per the law of large numbers states that with more than 30,000 mutual funds in existence, there will always be a few thousand in any given time period that will, in fact, outperform the markets. The question you have to ask yourself is: Do you think anyone— you or your advisers--can consistently and predictably identify which of those 15% are now poised to over-perform over the next decade? Remember: past victories do not correlate to future success.

**Finally, the third myth is market timing.** One of the most destructive myths is the belief that there is a measurable way to effectively get in and out of the market.

If only you sold all stocks January of 2008 (the peak) and fully invested back into the market in March of 2009 (the bottom) you would have had experienced tremendous growth. Wouldn't it be great if you could miss all the bear markets and corrections, then get right back in for the recoveries and bull markets?

Most of us recognize that with over 6 billion people on the planet making daily decisions, it is a mathematical anomaly to be able to do this over your entire lifetime as an investor. Market movements are simply too unpredictable, with millions of simultaneous inputs driving market pricing on a second to second basis, there is no amount of research or intelligence that can consistently project future market pricing.

With only new and unknowable information changing the market landscape, there's no way to predict. Those who are attempting to do so are executing nothing more than a "strategy" hinged on guesses and speculations.

Day traders - those who jump in and out of the market, on daily basis – are extreme examples of market timers. Market timing is defined as any attempt to change or alter your mix of assets based on a prediction about the future, and often times market timing manifests itself in a much more subtle and widespread fashion.

There are viable reasons for changing your financial plan or mix of assets. Maybe you want to retire sooner, you have a health condition, or you want to travel more. When your objectives and time horizons change, you may also need to adjust your financial plan to maintain an alignment between your goals and strategies. However, when you change your investment strategy based upon ideas that start with, "I think, I heard, I read, I suspect, my adviser thinks, an economist said, the media said, Jim Cramer said" - and the list goes on and on and on - you in fact, are market timing because you are changing your strategy based upon a prediction.

Market timing has unfortunately been one of the primary contributors to the average American earning less than 4% per year over the past 30-years, while large U.S. Stocks have earned over 10% annually. No wonder Americans are lukewarm on the stock market and skeptical about capitalism as whole. Imagine if everyone walking the streets of America had earned over 10% per year on their money for the last 30 years. What sort of dreams would they be able to accomplish? What would their overall perception be about the stock market and its role in wealth creation?

You see, as I mentioned earlier, the biggest threat to your investments is yourself. These three myths present the greatest basis for these slip-ups. If you're like others, you may mistake activity for control.

As a result, when you spend several hours researching the past performance of money managers and stocks, you aim to determine which investments to buy in the future. You make trades to get in and out of the market because the activity soothes your emotions and your anxiety. You gain a false sense of hope that you're in control of your money when in fact the data shows that you're destroying your potential for success and returns every time you try to adjust your investments by stock picking, track-record investing, or market timing.

Important note: These myths of destruction are exacerbated by commission-driven "advisers" who make money every time you move your investments from one to another. A disciplined strategy rooted in academics and a curbing of your emotions is essential to combat these brokers.

When you learn to avoid these myths, you not only improve your level of success, but you simultaneously cost traditional financial advisers and brokers billions of dollars. They are so financially threatened by you remaining disciplined that they will stop at nothing to play on your emotions and pressure you to market-time. This destructive conflict of interest in an "adviser" relationship, referenced earlier in the book, has incentivized many professionals to believe and perpetuate these myths. The result is them playing off of your emotions in an attempt to line their own pockets and erode your potential returns.

## Chapter #9—End of Chapter Questions

Do you stock pick, track record invest, or market time?

_____

_____

_____

If so, which ones and in what capacity?

_____

_____

_____

_____

_____

_____

_____

_____

_____

_____

_____

_____

# Conclusion:
# What does this mean for you?

You now have nine arrows in your quiver! NINE ways to UNLEASH your investments. What does this actually mean for you? How can you improve your situation with this knowledge?

*Knowing something is meaningless. Knowledge without action is nothing at all.*

To find investment success, you must stick to these principles. Even more though, you will need to find someone who can hold you accountable to following these rules. Remember, the first obstacle in maximizing your legacy is procrastination.

*How do you get started?*

Finding a good financial coach who can reinforce these rules is absolutely critical. That coach should embody the characteristics and qualifications as defined earlier in the book.

I want to make to make a special offer to you. At Keystone Wealth Partners, we are an independent, fee-only Registered Investment Advisory Firm that provides independent, objective advice.

People do not always know who to turn to for help with these financial matters and you may not either.

At Keystone, we are committed to helping you understand and learn these nine principles, along with many others. This book is one avenue, and another is through our ongoing commitment to client education.

Because you took the time to read my book, I'd like to offer you our One-Page Retirement Map Review. Perhaps you heard about this retirement map as explained on my weekly radio shows. It is called the Retirement Map Review because your entire financial situation is outlined on one page. Often your Retirement Map Review is the first time you have seen a simple, understandable snapshot of your entire situation from a true financial adviser as defined in this book. Your concerns and objectives are reflected on the map, along with our recommendations of how you can make improvements.

This initial review reveals the answer nearly everyone approaching retirement or who is already retired asks: "Will I be okay in retirement? Do I have enough money?"

You will receive your tailored retirement income projection in black and white. Then, and likely even more importantly, you will have the question answered of what rate of return you need to achieve your most important goals. Your Retirement Map Review will also include a stress test on your portfolio. This is where we crunch all of your accounts together and back-test them in times of crisis and volatility to ensure that no matter what comes your way, you and your family will be okay.

If we identify there are trouble spots, we will offer you some suggestions of how you can remove the risk in your portfolio to ensure that you and your family will not be put in a bind regardless of how long you live, and no matter what happens on the financial landscape.

Here's the best part. This is ALL completely free of charge. We are a mature firm, and this means there is no pressure from our team. We've performed this review for hundreds of people just like you. Some have become ongoing clients, and some have not. The one thing we know is that all who have seen their Retirement Review Map walk away feeling more confident and clearer about their retirement picture than ever before.

Thank you for reading my book. I hope you will take my offer seriously. My team and I would love to help you transform your legacy!

---

## *Unleash Your Investments*

## *9 Simple Truths to Transform Your Legacy*

---

# Nuggets of Truth:

In addition to the 9 Truths to Transform Your Legacy, here are a few more quick hitters for good measure. The next time you're considering a change in your investment strategy it's important that you revisit these gems to help avoid destructive behavior.

*"Most investors, both institutional and individual, will find that the best way to own common stocks is through an index fund that charges minimal fees. Those following this path are sure to beat the net results (after fees and expenses) delivered by the great majority of investment professionals."*

*-Warren Buffett, Chairman and CEO, Berkshire Hathaway, Inc.*

If Warren Buffet, arguably the world's greatest "stock picker", is urging you to NOT buy individual stocks but rather own stocks via index funds…he may have a point.

> *"There are two kinds of forecasters: those who don't know, and those who don't know they don't know."*

> *-John Kenneth Galbraith, economist and professor of economics at Harvard University*

No one has a crystal ball, and if they did, they wouldn't need to be soliciting you to pay $29 per month for their financial newsletter.

> *"When you look at the results on an after-fee, after-tax basis over reasonably long periods of time, there's almost no chance that you end up beating an index fund."*
> *(He went on to say the odds are 100 to 1)*
>
> *-David Swensen,*
> *Chief Investment Officer,*
> *Yale Endowment Fund*

Why anyone owns active, expensive mutual funds anymore is beyond me. Even worse, how advisers selling active mutual funds are able to sleep at night is even more perplexing.

> *"The statistical evidence proving that stock index funds outperform between 80% and 90% of actively managed equity funds is so overwhelming that it takes enormously expensive advertising campaigns to obscure the truth from investors."*
>
> *- The Motley Fool*

The media destroys investors' "American Dream" by exploiting natural human emotions.

*"If there's anything in the whole world of mutual funds that you can take to the bank, it's that expense ratios help you make a better decision. In every single time period and data point tested, low-cost funds beat high-cost funds."*

*- Russel Kinnel, Director of Mutual Fund Research, Morningstar, Inc.*

Own low-cost funds. It's that simple.

> *"The grim irony of investing, then, is that we investors as a group not only don't get what we pay for, we get precisely what we don't pay for. So if we pay for nothing, we get everything."*

> *- John C. Bogle, Founder and Retired CEO of The Vanguard Group*

Mutual funds are strange, there is often an inverse correlation between cost and long-term performance. This means we greatly increase our performance by owning lower-cost investments.

*"We have long felt that the only value of stock forecasters is to make fortune-tellers look good."*

*- Warren Buffett, Chairman and CEO, Berkshire Hathaway, Inc.*

The next time a talking head starts telling you what is going to happen next week in the market based upon the shape of a chart, chuckle and turn the channel.

> *"It must be apparent to intelligent investors that if anyone possessed the ability to do so [forecast the immediate trend of stock prices] consistently and accurately he would become a billionaire so quickly he would not find it necessary to sell his stock market guesses to the general public."*
>
> *- David L. Babson, Founder, Babson Capital Management*

If your financial adviser EVER recommends you make a change because of what they "think" is going to happen next, run, don't walk to the nearest exit of their office.

*"Most people think they can find managers who can outperform, but most people are wrong. Eighty-five percent to ninety percent of managers fail to match their benchmarks. Because managers have fees and incur transaction costs, you know that in the aggregate they are deleting value. The investment business is a giant scam."*

*- Jack Meyer, Former President, Harvard Management Company (which manages the $32B Harvard University Endowment)*

"Scam" may feel like a strong word, but as a "Reformed Broker" myself, I think it might be too kind.

*"Over the long-term the superiority of indexing is a mathematical certainty."*

*- Jason Zweig,*
*Author and Wall Street columnist*

If you want to play the odds, you invest using low-cost index funds. If instead you think you can find a needle in a haystack consistently over a 75-year period another strategy may be more suitable.

> *"Far more money has been lost by investors preparing for corrections, or trying to anticipate corrections, than has been lost in corrections themselves."*
>
> *- Peter Lynch, Former Manager, Fidelity Magellan Fund (and legendary investor)*

From 2009 to 2018 I met with countless investors who were fully out of the market to ensure they wouldn't be hurt in a crash or bear market. All they actually ensured was that they would miss out on the next 300% run up.

> *"If I have noticed anything over these 60 years on Wall Street, it is that people do not succeed in forecasting what's going to happen to the stock market."*
>
> *- Benjamin Graham, American economist and father of value investing*

No one has ever proven to be able to do it consistently and predictably over long periods of time, yet their lies still persist, and we want more than anything to believe they're true – and in turn can bring us closer to feeling in "control".

*After receiving the Nobel Prize, Daniel Kahneman was asked by a CNBC anchorman what investment tips he had for viewers. His answer: "Buy and hold."*

*- Daniel Kahneman, Professor at Princeton University and winner of the 2002 Nobel Prize in Economic Sciences*

Large United States Stocks have earned over 10% per year since 1926…if you simply bought and held. That would be north of 6% more per year than average American has earned the past 30 years on their stock mutual funds – according to Dalbar, Inc.

*"Even fierce resistance can be overcome. Low-transaction-cost index funds have benefited — very substantially — from slowly spreading knowledge of how hard-pressed stock-pickers are to best dart-throwing chimps and other mindless algorithms."*

*- Philip E. Tetlock,
Leonore Annenberg University
Professor of Psychology,
University of Pennsylvania*

The cat is out of the bag. No one can pick the "right" investments – not even your broker who takes your buddies and you out golfing.

> *"It is paradoxical that wealth is often created through investment concentration, but maintained through diversification and careful management."*

> *- Brad Berggren,*
> *Managing Director & Founder,*
> *Parametric Risk Advisors*

Most accumulate the bulk of their savings through wages, business ventures, entrepreneurship, real estate, and other saturated sources, but when looking at retirement, there is no more effective way to create efficiency and safety than through broad diversification.

> *"...I believe the best investment strategy for most investors is not to buy and sell stocks at all, but simply to allocate assets to low-cost passive funds. I didn't use to believe this. When I worked on Wall Street, it seemed absurd to think that the massive amount of energy, brainpower, and money expended on buying 'good' stocks and selling 'bad' ones was usually wasted (or worse). In the years since leaving the business, however, I have examined the evidence, and I have been startled and disappointed to realize how conclusive it is."*
>
> *- Henry Blodget,*
> *former equity research analyst*
> *at Prudential, Oppenheimer & Co.,*
> *and Merrill Lynch*

Even the brightest minds on Wall Street eventually come to terms with the reality.

*"The inconvenience of going from rich to poor is greater than most people can tolerate. Staying rich requires an entirely different approach from getting rich. It might be said that one gets rich by working hard and taking big risks, and that one stays rich by limiting risk and not spending too much."*

*- Peter L. Bernstein & Aswath Damodaran, quote from their book Investment Management This mental paradigm shift is one that many investors struggle with accepting as they near and enter retirement.*

Even the brightest minds on Wall Street eventually come to terms with the reality.

> *"Perhaps the easiest financial product to sell is one that offers safety plus a high yield. Of course, the product may only offer the illusion of safety plus a high yield (safety plus a high yield being rather hard to obtain). But that won't stop it selling well.*
> *Often very well."*
>
> *- John Hempton,*
> *Chief Investment Officer,*
> *Bronte Capital Management*

If it sounds too good to be true, it probably is. Case in point, the variable annuity. I have yet to find a policy holder who actually understands what they were so aggressively sold.

*"In money management what sells
is the illusion of certainty."*

*- John Hempton,
Chief Investment Officer,
Bronte Capital Management*

Investors will look to relieve anxiety by seeking a sense of security. Whether in reality it is a false sense of security or not only matters on paper.

*"In investing, what is comfortable
is rarely profitable."*

*- Robert Arnott*

At times, you will have to step out of your comfort zone
to realize significant gains. Know the boundaries of your
comfort zone and practice stepping out of it in small
doses. As much as you need to know the market, you need
to know yourself too. Can you handle staying in when
everyone else is jumping ship? Or getting out during the
biggest rally of the century? There's no room for pride in
this kind of self-analysis. The best investment strategy can
turn into the worst if you don't have the stomach to see it
through.

*"How many millionaires do you
know who have become wealthy
by investing in savings accounts?
I rest my case."*

*- Robert G. Allen*

Though investing in a savings account is a sure bet, your gains will be minimal given the extremely low interest rates. But don't forgo one completely. A savings account is a reliable place for an emergency fund, whereas a market investment is not.

*"The individual investor should act consistently as an investor and not as a speculator."*
*- Ben Graham*

You are an investor, not someone who can predict the future. Base your decisions on real facts and analysis rather than risky, speculative forecasts.

> *"Investing should be more like watching paint dry or watching grass grow. If you want excitement, take $800 and go to Las Vegas."*
>
> *- Paul Samuelson*

If you think investing is gambling, you're doing it wrong. The work involved requires planning and patience. However, the gains you see over time are indeed exciting!

*"The four most dangerous words in investing are: 'this time it's different.'"*

*- Sir John Templeton*

*"Follow market trends and history. Don't speculate that this particular time will be any different. For example, a major key to investing in a particular stock or bond fund is its performance over five years. Nothing shorter."*

*- Seth Klarman*

# Buffett's Only Two Rules For Investing…

---

*"Rule No. 1: Never lose money.*
*Rule No. 2: Never forget rule No.1"*

*- Warren Buffett*

---

## High Returns With Low Risk is the Key

---

*"Risk comes from not knowing what you are doing."*

*- Warren Buffett*

---

## Get Around the Right People

*"It's better to hang out with people better than you. Pick out associates whose behavior is better than yours and you'll drift in that direction."*

*- Warren Buffett*

## Invest for the Long Term

---

*"Only buy something that you'd be perfectly happy to hold if the market shut down for 10 years."*

*- Warren Buffett*

---

# Doing Nothing is Often the Right Thing to Do

---

*"You do things when the opportunities come along. I've had periods in my life when I've had a bundle of ideas come along, and I've had long dry spells. If I get an idea next week, I'll do something. If not, I won't do a damn thing."*

*- Warren Buffett*

---

## Appreciate Where You Came From

> *"Someone's sitting in the shade today because someone planted a tree a long time ago."*
>
> *- Warren Buffett*

## Give Back to Society

*"If you're in the luckiest 1% of humanity, you owe it to the rest of humanity to think about the other 99%."*

*- Warren Buffett*

## Don't Make Investing Difficult

> *"There seems to be some perverse human characteristic that likes to make easy things difficult."*
>
> *- Warren Buffett*

# Make Your Own Forecasts

*"Forecasts may tell you a great deal about the forecaster; they tell you nothing about the future."*

*- Warren Buffett*

## History Doesn't Dictate the Future

*"If past history was all that is needed to play the game of money, the richest people would be librarians."*

*- Warren Buffett*

## History Doesn't Dictate the Future

---

*"I will tell you how to become rich. Close the doors. Be fearful when others are greedy. Be greedy when others are fearful."*

*- Warren Buffett*

---

## Buy It Thinking You Will Hold It Forever

---

*"Our favorite holding period*
*is forever."*

*- Warren Buffett*

---

*"While it might seem that anyone can be a value investor, the essential characteristics of this type of investor-patience, discipline, and risk aversion-may well be genetically determined."*

*- Seth Klarman*

*"The stock market is the story of cycles and of the human behavior that is responsible for overreactions in both directions."*

*- Seth Klarman*

*"Generally, the greater the stigma or revulsion, the better the bargain."*

*- Seth Klarman*

*"Investing is the intersection of economics and psychology."*

*- Seth Klarman*

*"Value investing is at its core the marriage of a contrarian streak and a calculator."*

*- Seth Klarman*

*"While some might mistakenly consider value investing a mechanical tool for identifying bargains, it is actually a comprehensive investment philosophy that emphasizes the need to perform in-depth fundamental analysis, pursue long-term investment results, limit risk, and resist crowd psychology."*

*- George Soros*

*"If investing is entertaining, if you're having fun, you're probably not making any money. Good investing is boring."*

*- George Soros*

# About The Author
## John Hagensen

When it comes to being a pilot, ensuring a safe flight requires the unique ability to decisively adapt as conditions emerge. It is this kind of precision and attention to detail that make John Hagensen not only an exceptional pilot, but have also led him to build one of the state's most respected financial planning firms. *

John Hagensen is the Founder and Managing Director of Keystone Wealth Partners. His vision for starting KWP was to deliver financial planning strategies free from Wall Street's embedded conflicts of interest. Today, clients benefit from these strategies targeted to meet their unique needs.

His thought-leadership is driven by his desire to find new and interesting ways to educate investors. Having the heart of a teacher, his approach is educational and consultative. He is passionate about coaching his clients to remain disciplined to a long-term, academically-sound strategy and executes this through monthly group coaching sessions. His intention to inform Main Street Investors is also demonstrated through his weekly radio show, "Myth Busting with Keystone Wealth Partners" as well as his weekly podcast "Rethink Your Money". John is a sought-after public speaker and has educated thousands nearing retirement across the valley. In addition, John is a published author. His book, "Unleash Your Investments" hit shelves in the summer of 2017. He is a regular contributor to National Publication, including Forbes, Yahoo Finance and Bankrate.com.

John has a Master of Science Degree in Financial Services from the Institute of Business & Finance, a Strategic Decision and Risk Management Professional Certification from Stanford University, and a Behavioral Finance Professional Certificate from Duke University. John holds the credentials of Certified Funds Specialist (CFS), Certified

Annuity Specialist (CAS), Certified Estate & Trust Specialist (CES), Certified Tax Specialist (CTS), and Certified Income Specialist (CIS). John holds a designation from the National Social Security Association (NSSA) and completed his undergraduate Bachelor of Science degree at Corban University.

John is a native of Washington state, and currently resides in Gilbert with his wife, Brittany, and their five children. He has many passions, but none more than adoption and social-justice. After 4 trips to Ethiopia while adopting two of their children, sustainable, clean-water projects in Africa became a primary focus for John and his wife. John leads a community Bible Study, and believes his faith is the central anchor to every component of his life and business.

He also loves all-things sports, and as a child had every NBA player's number and college attended memorized. After attending a match while in Spain, he was hooked and is a devoted Barcelona FC soccer fan. More than sports or business though, his greatest joy lies in his family. His left shoulder is sore most days from throwing countless pass routes with his two football-obsessed teenagers, and he can recite every page of "Go-Dogs-Go". He is an avid reader and will knock out 50 non-fiction books in a typical year. As a Seattle native, he drinks more coffee than virtually anyone on earth, and his future goals include learning to speak Spanish fluently, become a capable pianist, and continuing to run at least one marathon per year.

Made in the USA
Lexington, KY
06 December 2019